# ON SECOND
# THOUGHT...

# ON SECOND THOUGHT...

## 365 OF THE WORST PROMISES, PREDICTIONS, AND PRONOUNCEMENTS EVER MADE!

### GARY BELSKY

Adams Media Corporation
Holbrook, Massachusetts

Published by
Adams Media Corporation
260 Center Street, Holbrook, MA 02343

ISBN: 1-58062-055-8

Printed in Canada.

J I H G F E D C B A

Library of Congress Cataloging-in-Publications Data
Belsky, Gary.
On second thought : 365 promises, predictions, and pronouncements
that never should have been made (by people who should have known
better) / by Gary Belsky.
    p.    cm.
Includes bibliographical references.
ISBN 1-58062-055-8
1. Quotations, English.  2. Celebrities—Quotations.  I. Title.
    PN6081.B36        1998
    082—DC21          98-7382
                      CIP

*This book is available at quantity discounts for bulk purchases.
For information, call 1-800-872-5627
(in Massachusetts, 781-767-8100).*

**Visit our home page at http://www.adamsmedia.com**

To my old friend Josh Kosowsky,
who predicted that this book
would never be published

*and*

To my nephews and niece—
Ari, Mo, Adir, Sam, Zevi, and Elly—
whom I've loved since they were born,
without second thought.

# Contents

# Introduction

Eating crow. Eating your words. Foot-in-mouth disease. By any name, we've all experienced it: a promise made, a prediction proffered, or a pronouncement intoned that not only turned out to be false but helped us look like complete fools in the process. This book is an attempt to collect of some of the more famous—and infamous—of these verbal miscues in history, ranging from serious miscalculations about life and death to sublime errors about love and romance. It's meant to inform and entertain, but if it helps you feel better about your own verbal gaffes, so much the better.

# 1

# *Isn't It Romantic?*

**Misguided musings about love and marriage**

*"I love him better every day."*

> Elizabeth Taylor, 1950, just after marrying her first husband, hotel baron Conrad Hilton.

*"I just want to be with him, to be his wife."*

> Elizabeth Taylor, 1952, just before marrying her second husband, actor Michael Wilding.

*"Thirty or forty years."*

Elizabeth Taylor, 1959, predicting the length of her honeymoon to fourth husband, singer Eddie Fisher. (Her third husband, Michael Todd, died in a plane crash one year after their 1957 marriage.)

*"This marriage will last forever."*

Elizabeth Taylor, 1964, at her marriage to fifth husband Richard Burton, whom she divorced in 1974.

*"We are stuck together like chicken feathers to tar."*

> Elizabeth Taylor, 1975, discussing her remarriage to Richard Burton, which lasted a year.

*"I have never been so happy."*

> Elizabeth Taylor, 1976, soon after marrying Senator John Warner.

*"This is it, forever."*

> Elizabeth Taylor, 1991, announcing her marriage to Larry Fortensky, which ended in 1995.

*"If any couple is in love, they'll have a happy marriage and no amount of gossip will ever break it up."*

> Movie starlet Janet Leigh, 1953, denying reports that her marriage to Tony Curtis was in trouble. The couple divorced in 1962.

*"Don't pay any attention to any of the drivel you hear about me and Jack Kennedy. It doesn't mean a thing."*

Jackie Bouvier, 1952, to then-fiancé John Husted. A year later she married Kennedy.

*"If you love a girl, you love her forever."*

Bodybuilder Mickey Hargitay, 1963, after reconciling with ex-wife, the actress Jayne Mansfield. Within a year they had divorced again for good.

*"I got you babe."*

> Husband and wife song team Sonny and Cher, 1965–1974, who sang their hit song at the end of each episode of their weekly variety show—until the show was canceled in the wake of their 1974 divorce.

*"I finally found a broad I can cheat on."*

> Frank Sinatra, 1966, praising his new wife, Mia Farrow. Within a year and a half he filed for divorce.

*"Rod will stay with me—forever."*

Actress Britt Ekland, 1976, on her husband, rock star Rod Stewart. Forever lasted a year before the couple divorced in 1977.

*"When elected, Newt will keep his family together."*

Ad for Congressman Newt Gingrich's first congressional campaign, 1978. Less than two years later, Gingrich filed for divorce.

*"I couldn't have married any other kind of woman."*

Prince Charles, 1991, on his doomed marriage to Lady Diana Spencer. Perhaps he should have.

*"Now I have what I always wanted . . . I have my knight in shining armor."*

Former Miss America Phyllis George, 1981, on her marriage to Kentucky governor John Y. Brown Jr. By 1996, the armor had rusted and the Browns divorced.

*"I resolve if I ever get hit in the face again with rice, it will be because I insulted a Chinese person."*

Talk show host Johnny Carson, 1984, vowing never to get married again after the end of his third marriage, and before the beginning of his fourth.

*"Where I am now is where I will remain for the rest of my life. The family is solid."*

Actress Jane Fonda, 1984, on her marriage to Tom Hayden. Fonda is now wed to media mogul Ted Turner.

*"I simply want to be a family man."*

Singer Elton John, 1984, upon his marriage to sound engineer Renate Blauel. The couple divorced four years later, and John soon after announced to no surprise that he was, in fact, gay.

*"It's so wonderful at last to have found someone to look after me."*

Sarah, Duchess of York, 1986, on her ill-fated marriage to Prince Andrew.

*". . . the coolest guy in the universe."*

Album dedication from Madonna, 1986, to
her husband, the actor Sean Penn, less
than three years before she filed for divorce.

*"I feel like Cinderella. I married Prince
Charming."*

Actress Loni Anderson, 1988, upon
marrying actor Burt Reynolds, whom she
divorced in a bitter fight five years later.

*"I just tore up my address book."*

Rolling Stones guitarist Bill Wyman, 1989, on his commitment to new bride Mandy Smith, a year before the couple began divorce proceedings.

*"I'm married to the greatest man in the world."*

Designer Carolyne Roehm, 1990, on her husband, tycoon Henry Kravis, three years before their divorce.

*"I just knew she was the one for me. My happiness is complete."*

Charles, the 9th Earl Spencer, circa 1990, on his reason for asking model Victoria Lockwood to marry him after knowing her just ten days. They later separated.

*"This is what we call paradise."*

Actor Cotter Smith, 1990, on his wedded bliss with actress Mel Harris. Paradise ended in 1996.

*"Why go looking when you already have exactly what you want?"*

Tycoon Donald Trump, summer 1991, on his reconciliation with girlfriend Marla Maples.

*"It's the end of an era."*

Donald Trump, fall 1991, on breaking up with Marla Maples again, before getting back together with her two weeks later. The couple eventually married, but filed for divorce in 1997.

*"This is completely right."*

Actress Julia Roberts, 1993, on her twenty-one-month marriage to singer Lyle Lovett.

*"Christie Brinkley loves me now. What else do I need?"*

Singer Billy Joel, 1993, a year before he and Brinkley split up.

*". . . it really is like Cinderella."*

Pop music star Mariah Carey, 1993, on her marriage to record mogul Tommy Mottola. Four years later she split from Prince Charming.

*"He's always been the fun I never had in my life."*

Actress Roseanne Barr, March 1993, describing husband Tom Arnold—before the fun ended and she divorced him.

*"I care about being with my husband. I take my marriage seriously."*

Actress Shannen Doherty, January 1994—four months after marrying actor Ashley Hamilton, and three months before filing for divorce.

*"[Martin] is like my brother."*

Actress Tisha Campbell, 1994, describing her Fox television costar Martin Lawrence, two years before she filed charges accusing him of sexual harassment.

*"The best thing I've ever done in my whole life."*

Actress Pamela Anderson Lee, 1995, on her marriage to rock star Tommy Lee, a year before filing for divorce. Anderson Lee changed her mind again—and then again, filing for divorce in February 1998.

*"Incredibly monogamous."*

Opera singer Luciano Pavarotti, October 1995, describing his marriage to Adua Pavarotti. Less than half a year later Pavarotti admitted to having an affair with a twenty-six-year-old assistant.

*"[Billy Bob Thornton] would never do anything to make me question the integrity of our marriage."*

Actress Pietra Dawn Thornton, 1996, a year before she filed for divorce from director Thornton and requested that a restraining order be placed against him.

*"I've found the person I'm complete with."*

Actress Gwyneth Paltrow, fall 1996, discussing her soon-to-be fiancé Brad Pitt. Less than a year later the couple had broken up.

# 2

# *Monkey Business*

**Daffy delusions about dollars and sense**

*"The wealth of the South is permanent and real, that of the North fugitive and fictitious."*

> *Debow's Review* editorial, 1857, four years before the Civil War and eight years before the South was in financial ruin.

*"There has never been a time in our history when work was so abundant, or when wages were as high."*

> President Grover Cleveland, January 1893. Within months the country was in the throes of depression.

*"The horse is here to stay, but the automobile is only a novelty—a fad."*

The president of the Michigan Savings Bank advising Henry Ford's lawyer Horace Rackham not to invest in the Ford Motor Company, 1903.

*"We still continue to enjoy a literally unprecedented prosperity."*

President Theodore Roosevelt, December 1906, less than three months before the start of the Financial Panic of 1907.

*"The Federal Reserve System will materially check undue expansion by making banks conservative as to their loans."*

Charles Hamilton, first governor of the Federal Reserve Board, December 1914. Fifteen years later, speculative loan policies by U.S. banks contributed to the Great Stock Market Crash of 1929.

*"We may look with confidence to the progress of business in 1929."*

International Business Machines founder Thomas Watson, 1928, less than a year before the stock market crashed and the country swooned into depression.

*"Stock prices have reached what looks like a permanently high plateau."*

Yale University economics professor Irving Fisher, 1929, just months before the Great Stock Market Crash.

*"Now everybody will get back to work."*

General Motors president Alfred P. Sloan, October 1929, before the worst depression in U.S. history.

*"I think there is a world market for about five computers."*

IBM chairman Thomas Watson, 1943.

*"The Edsel is here to stay."*

Henry Ford II, 1957, two years before Ford Motor Company stopped producing the disastrous Edsel sedan.

*"The concept is interesting and well-formed, but in order to earn better than a 'C' the idea must be feasible."*

Yale University management professor's comment on a paper written by Fred Smith proposing an overnight delivery service, circa early 1970s. Smith went on to start Federal Express.

*"What's it good for?"*

Intel chairman and cofounder Gordon Moore, early 1970s, when presented with the idea for personal computers.

*"This is like trying to buy a ticket on the Titanic."*

New York real estate developer Fred Trump, 1976, on his son Donald's plan to buy the failing Commodore Hotel in Manhattan. In fact, the successful deal launched The Donald's career.

*"There is no reason for any individual to have a computer in their home."*

Digital Equipment president Ken Olsen, 1977.

*"The Death of Equities."*

*Business Week* magazine cover, 1979, three years before the start of the biggest bull market in history.

*"The in-depth preliminary investigations and the involvement of the brokerage community in tax investments have dramatically improved the quality of the product in the last few years."*

James Darr, director of tax investments at Bache Halsey Stuart Shields, November 1980. Darr became Prudential Bache's top partnership executive, and wound up enmeshed in one of the worst Wall Street scandals in history.

*"This book is intended to explain an activity that has been hidden from public view for no good reason. Undue profits are not made; there are no esoteric tricks that enable arbitrageurs to outwit the system."*

Stock arbitrageur and author Ivan Boesky in his 1985 book *Merger Mania*. Shortly thereafter he was convicted of, and jailed for, such esoteric tricks as insider trading.

*"The most significant soft drink development in the company's history. The best has been made even better."*

Coca-Cola chairman Roberto Goizueta, 1985, on New Coke®. It was pulled from store shelves three months later.

*"Drexel is like a god . . . and a god can do anything it wants."*

Framed quote in the office of investment banker and Drexel Burnham Lambert employee Stephen Weinroth, circa 1986. Within four years Drexel was out of business.

**" "**

*"The force in this country buying high-yield securities [junk bonds] has overpowered all regulation."*

Wall Street financier and junk bond king Michael Milken, 1986, less than four years before government regulation overpowered and sent him to prison.

*"No ifs, ands, or buts, Lou, it's going up."*

Financial pundit Dan Dorfman to CNN anchor Lou Dobbs, October 1987—the night before a four-day, 769-point slide in the stock market.

*"What we do have is a strong feeling about the ability and integrity of John Gutfreund . . . I like, admire and trust John."*

Berkshire Hathaway chairman Warren Buffett, 1987, referring to the head of the investment bank Salomon Brothers. Four years later Gutfreund was sacked in disgrace.

*"When will the next, much broader [financial] crisis begin? In 1989, probably in February or March of 1989."*

Former banker Paul Erdman, in his 1988 book *What's Next? How to Prepare Yourself for the Crash of '89 and Profit in the 1990s.* No such crash happened.

*"If the [Texas savings and loan] industry is to survive, its member institutions must take positive steps to rebuild public confidence by instituting strict codes of ethical business conduct."*

American Federal Bank chairman William E. Gibson, 1989, three years before he was convicted in federal court of fraud.

*"[Tonya] Harding and her down-home All-American appeal and charm will knock the winter socks off many Americans. Add to this that she is a young woman and happily married and you have an excellent spokesperson for family oriented products and services."*

Press release from the consulting firm Sports Marketing Group, October 1991.

*"Running a business these days is like running a marathon . . . you have to have a strategy for how to run the whole race, so that you don't . . . fade at the finish."*

RJR Nabisco chairman Louis Gerstner, in the company's 1992 annual report. Within months Gerstner left RJR Nabisco to take the top spot at IBM.

*"[I am] prepared to be a full-time chairman of Apple. I am not walking away from Apple. I have no plans to go anywhere else."*

Apple Computer chairman John Sculley, June 1993, four months before quitting his post to take another job.

*"It was a gem that fell into my lap."*

Former Apple chairman John Sculley, October 1993, describing his decision to take over tiny Spectrum Technologies—four months before resigning from the company.

*"This is the business I've been working in for twenty-eight years, and we're just getting to the point where we're realizing the dreams we had many years ago. It's just the wrong time to get out of this business."*

Motorola chief executive officer George Fisher, September 1993. A month later he accepted the top job at Eastman Kodak.

*"Despite a massive tax increase, the end of the Cold War, and pickup in the economy, the federal budget deficit is not going down."*

T. Rowe Price economist Paul Boltz, December 1993. In fact, the federal budget deficit in fiscal 1994 declined by $52 billion.

*"We are looking for the price of gold reaching better than $500 an ounce sometime in early 1995."*

Kemper Securities gold analyst Vahid Fathi, April 1994. He's still waiting.

*"Robert L. Citron's winning record as Orange County's treasurer–tax collector is good enough that he deserves reelection."*

*Los Angeles Times* editorial, May 1994, less than a year before Orange County filed for bankruptcy protection and Citron resigned as treasurer–tax collector.

*"We think GE is unlikely to try selling Kidder Peabody right away."*

Argus research report, October 1994. One week later, General Electric agreed to sell its Kidder Peabody brokerage to PaineWebber for $670 million.

*"We think the healthy, good-for-you beverage categories are going to continue to grow."*

Quaker Oats chairman William Smithburg, November 1994, upon the company's purchase of Snapple Beverage for $1.7 billion. Less than three years later Quaker sold Snapple for $300 million, or a $1.4 billion loss.

*"The newly elected Congress has not yet convened, but it is already time for the Republicans to think seriously about how they are going to handle the recession of 1996."*

Economist John M. Mueller, December 1994, predicting a recession that never came.

*"It's difficult to see how stocks can move much higher."*

Former Lehman Brothers market strategist Katherine Hensel, January 1995. In fact, stock prices increased more than 20 percent that year and the next.

*"We must issue a strong warning about mutual funds. By the end of 1995, mutual funds will be the most despised investments."*

Financial talk show hosts and authors Ken and Daria Dolan, February 1995.

*"I am especially gratified to be able to have an additional partner going forward to manage this great and complex entertainment company. There's plenty for the two of us to do."*

Disney chairman Michael Eisner, August 1995, commenting on the hiring of superagent Michael Ovitz as company president. Within eighteen months Ovitz resigned and Eisner called his hiring a mistake.

*"America Online is likely to be a $100 stock by year end. In a field encumbered by hype and jargon, AOL beats the competition by offering an easy-to-use interface."*

Morgan Stanley securities analyst Michael Sorell, 1995. By the end of the next year AOL was under fire for offering customers inconsistent access to the Internet.

# 3

# *Inexact Science*

Noteworthy nitwitticisms
about medicine, science,
and technology

*"Inventions reached their limit long ago, and I see no hope for further development."*

Julius Frontinus, first century A.D.

*"So many centuries after creation, it is unlikely that anyone could find hitherto unknown lands of any value."*

From a report presented to King Ferdinand and Queen Isabella of Spain, 1486, regarding Christopher Columbus's plan to search for a shorter route to the Indies.

*"The western ocean is infinite and perhaps unnavigable."*

From the same report, 1486.

*"Men might as well project a voyage to the moon as attempt to employ steam navigation against the stormy north Atlantic Ocean."*

Irish astronomer and philosopher professor Dionysius Lardner, 1838.

*"Rail travel at high speed is not possible, because passengers, unable to breathe, would die of asphyxia."*

> Irish astronomer, philosopher, and professor Dionysius Lardner, circa 1835.

*"Drill for oil? You mean drill into the ground and try to find oil? You're crazy!"*

> Response from drilling company executives to oil industry pioneer Edwin Drake, 1859.

*"Louis Pasteur's theory of germs is ridiculous fiction."*

> French professor of physiology Pierre Pachet, 1872.

*"The telephone has too many shortcomings to be seriously considered as a means of communication."*

> A corporate memo from telegraph operator Western Union, 1876.

**❝ ❞**

*"What use could this company make of an electric toy?"*

Western Union president William Orton, circa 1870s, turning down the chance to buy Alexander Graham Bell's patent for the telephone.

*"The abdomen, the chest, and the brain will forever be shut from the intrusion of the wise and humane."*

Sir John Eric Ericksen, surgeon-extraordinary to Queen Victoria of England, predicting in the early 1870s that surgery would never succeed.

"Railroads, water courses, telegraphs, telephones, pneumatic tubes, and all other methods of transporting passengers, freight, and intelligence will be owned and operated by the government."

Labor leader T. V. Powderly, 1893, predicting the role of government a hundred years in the future.

"*I presume that, in the next century, there may be built a railway reaching so far that it may be possible to enter a palace car in New York City and ride it to Lima, Santiago, Rio de Janeiro, or Buenos Aires.*"

Famed industrialist W. R. Grace, 1893.

"*Heavier-than-air flying machines are impossible.*"

British mathematician and physicist William Thomson Kelvin, 1895.

*"Everything that can be invented, has been invented."*

> U.S. Patent Office commissioner Charles Duell, 1899.

*"I must confess that my imagination . . . refuses to see any sort of submarine doing anything but suffocating its crew and floundering at sea."*

> British author and futurist H. G. Wells, 1901.

*"Man will not fly for fifty years."*

Aviation pioneer Wilbur Wright, 1901.

❝ ❞

*"The aeroplane will never fly."*

British minister of war Lord Haldane, 1907.

❝ ❞

*"Flight by machines heavier than air is unpractical and insignificant."*

Astronomer Simon Newcomb, 1907, eighteen months before the Wright brothers' first flight.

❝ ❞

"No flying machine will ever fly from New York to Paris."

Orville Wright, 1908.

"Airplanes are interesting toys but of no military value."

French military strategist Ferdinand Foch, 1911.

"The popular mind often pictures gigantic flying machines speeding across the Atlantic, carrying innumerable passengers. . . . Such ideas must be wholly visionary. Even if such a machine could get across with one or two passengers, it would be prohibitive to any but the capitalist who could own his own yacht."

Harvard astronomer William Pickering, 1913.

*"[Airmail is] an impractical sort of fad, and has no place in the serious job of postal transportation."*

Second Assistant U.S. Postmaster General Paul Henderson, 1922.

*"Professor Goddard . . . does not know the relation of action to reaction, and of the need to have something better than a vacuum against which to react. . . . Of course, he only seems to lack the knowledge ladled out daily in high schools."*

New York Times editorial, 1920, refuting the notion that rocketry pioneer Robert Goddard's inventions could actually travel in outer space.

"[Would it] not be well to exclude women from a field of activity in which [their] presence certainly is unnecessary from any point of view?"

New York Times editorial, 1921, on the question of whether women should be allowed to pilot planes.

*"The wireless music box has no imaginable commercial value. Who would pay for a message sent to nobody in particular?"*

Response from associates of RCA founder David Sarnoff, circa 1920s, when he proposed investing in the young radio industry.

*"This fellow Charles Lindbergh will never make it. He's doomed."*

Millionaire and aviation buff Harry Guggenheim, 1927, on Lindy's soon-to-be-successful solo flight across the Atlantic.

*"This foolish idea of shooting at the moon is an example of the absurd length to which vicious specialization will carry scientists working in thought-tight compartments."*

British scientist William Bickerton, 1929.

*"The most revolutionary war invention since the discovery of gunpowder."*

An article in the July 1932 issue of *Modern Mechanics*, describing plans to build a flying tank.

*"Anyone who expects a source of power from the transformation of the atom is talking moonshine."*

Nobel laureate and scientist Lord Rutherford, 1933.

*"Automobiles will start to decline almost as soon as the last shot is fired in World War II. . . . Instead of a car in every garage, there will be a helicopter."*

Aviation publicist Harry Bruno, 1943.

*"RAAF Captures Flying Saucer on Ranch in Roswell Region."*

Roswell Daily Record headline, July 8, 1945, one day before the newspaper retracted the fabled hoax.

**" "**

*"Computers in the future may weigh no more than 1.5 tons."*

Popular Mechanics, 1949.

*"Space travel is utter bilge."*

Richard van der Riet Woolley, royal astronomer and space adviser to the British government, 1956. A year later the Russians successfully launched the Sputnik satellite.

**6699**

*"I have traveled the length and breadth of this country and walked with the best people, and I can assure you that data processing is a fad that won't last out the year."*

Editor in charge of business books for publisher Prentice-Hall, 1957.

*"A few decades hence, energy may be free, just like the unmetered air."*

Atomic Energy Commission member John von Neumann, 1956, on the impact of nuclear power.

*"Man will never reach the moon regardless of all future scientific advances."*

Renowned scientist and inventor Lee De Forest, 1957, twelve years before Neil Armstrong stepped off *Apollo 9* and onto the moon.

*"For the majority of people, the use of tobacco has a beneficial effect."*

Los Angeles surgeon Ian MacDonald, 1963, as quoted in *Newsweek*.

*"But what good is it for?"*

Now-anonymous engineer at IBM, 1968, commenting on the recent invention of the microchip.

*"640K ought to be good enough for anybody."*

> Microsoft president Bill Gates, 1981, on the sufficiency of computer memory at the time.

# 4

# *Politically Incorrect*

### Galling gaffes about government and politics

*"One should not believe in conspiracies until they have attained their goal."*

Roman emperor Domitian, who was assassinated by conspiracists in 96 A.D.

*"The cheek of every American must tingle with shame as he reads the silly, flat, and dish-watery utterances of the man who has to be pointed out to intelligent foreigners as President of the United States."*

*Chicago Times* editorial, 1863, criticizing Abraham Lincoln's Gettysburg Address.

*"All of North America will be under one government, managed by a council consisting of a few men."*

Senator William A. Peffer, 1893, on how things would look in 1993.

*"In 1993, the government will have grown more simple."*

Poet Ella Wheeler Wilcox, 1893.

*"The election of president by an electoral college—which often turns the contest on a few pivotal states and sometimes thwarts the will of the people—is destined to be replaced by a more direct method of ascertaining the popular will."*

Three-time presidential candidate and noted Populist William Jennings Bryan, 1893, predicting changes in politics over the next hundred years.

*"Politically, there will be far less money expended in electing officials."*

Famed newspaper columnist Bill Nye, 1893, when asked to predict how the U.S. would look in 1993.

*"Sensible and responsible women do not want to vote."*

Former president Grover Cleveland, 1900, on the suffrage movement.

*"We have murder by the throat."*

British prime minister David Lloyd George, 1920, predicting a quick end to the troubles in Ireland.

*"Herbert Hoover is certainly a wonder, and I wish we could make him president. There couldn't be a better one."*

Franklin D. Roosevelt, 1920, four years before he ran for president—against Hoover.

*"I want to be an old-fashioned lawyer, an honest lawyer who can't be bought by crooks."*

Future president Richard Nixon, 1925, to his mother.

*"A pleasant man who, without any important qualifications for the office, would very much like to be President."*

Newspaper columnist Walter Lippmann, 1932, discussing future four-term president Franklin Delano Roosevelt.

*"FDR will be a one-term president."*

Newspaper columnist Mark Sullivan, 1935, on the chances of re-election of Franklin D. Roosevelt, who went on to win three more terms in office.

*"I have no political ambition for myself or for my children."*

Joseph P. Kennedy, 1936.

*"There is [sic] not enough troops in the army to force the Southern people to break down segregation and admit the Negro race into our theaters, into our swimming pools, and into our churches."*

Senator Strom Thurmond, 1948.

**" "**

*"Dewey Defeats Truman."*

*Chicago Tribune* headline, November 4, 1948. Actually, Truman defeated Dewey in that presidential election.

**" "**

*"Castro won't last a year."*

Cuban president Fulgencio Batista, 1957.

*"Television is not as effective as it once was."*

Presidential candidate Richard Nixon, assessing the significance of his televised debates with John F. Kennedy in 1960. Nixon's poor showing in the debates were thought to be his undoing in the election.

### *"The boy didn't win."*

Vice presidential nominee Lyndon B.
Johnson, assessing running mate JFK's
debate performance.

### *"Segregation now! Segregation tomorrow! Segregation forever."*

Alabama governor George Wallace, 1963,
less than nine months before Alabama
schools were integrated.

*"I promise that truth shall be the policy of the Nixon administration."*

Vice President Spiro Agnew, 1968.

*"Truth will become the hallmark of the Nixon administration."*

Director of communications, Executive Branch, U.S. Government, Herb Klein, 1969.

*"No woman will in my time be prime minister."*

British politician—and future prime minister—Margaret Thatcher, 1969.

**❝ ❞**

*"[I'm] 100 percent for Tom Eagleton . . . [I have] no intention of dropping him from the ticket."*

Senator and Democratic presidential candidate George McGovern, July 1972, denying that he would drop Eagleton as his vice presidential running mate. He dropped him days later.

**❝ ❞**

*"I'm not going to comment from the White House on a third-rate burglary attempt."*

> White House press secretary Ron Ziegler, 1972, commenting on the burglary of Democratic National Headquarters at the Watergate apartment building.

*"I applaud President Nixon's comprehensive statement which clearly demonstrates again that the president was not involved with the Watergate matter."*

> George Bush, 1974, less than six months before Nixon resigned.

*"The vice presidency is not much of a job."*

> Nelson Rockefeller, 1974, weeks before accepting Gerald Ford's offer to become vice president of the United States.

*"I don't want to be prime minister again. It's pretty tough going."*

> Indira Gandhi, 1974, shortly before she ran for and won the prime minister's job again.

*"An island of stability."*

President Jimmy Carter, 1979, describing
the shah of Iran, a few months before the
shah was overthrown.

*"I would like to suggest that Ronald
Reagan is politically dead."*

NBC political correspondent Tom Pettit,
January 1980.

## "As of now, I'm in control of the White House."

Secretary of State Alexander Haig, March 1981, after President Reagan was shot and while Vice President Bush was in transit. In fact, he wasn't in charge.

## "You know I once played Grover Cleveland in the movies."

Ronald Reagan, 1981, commenting on House Speaker Tip O'Neill's desk, which had belonged to President Cleveland. Reagan had actually portrayed Grover Cleveland *Alexander*, the baseball player.

*"If you don't believe me, just follow me."*

Presidential hopeful Gary Hart, 1988, denying reports that he was engaged in an adulterous affair. Reporters took his suggestion and discovered his relationship with Donna Rice.

*"Read my lips: No new taxes."*

George Bush, 1988, eighteen months before he raised taxes and four years before he lost the 1992 election to Bill Clinton.

*" . . . the fire of an election no longer burns in me."*

Arkansas governor Bill Clinton, 1990, explaining why he would not run again for public office.

**❝ ❞**

*"I want to say one thing to the American people. I want you to listen to me. I'm going to say this again: I did not have sexual relations with that woman, Miss Lewinsky."*

President Bill Clinton, January 26, 1998.

**❝ ❞**

*"I did have a relationship with Miss Lewinsky that was not appropriate. In fact, it was wrong."*

Clinton, eight months later.

**❝ ❞**

*"[The Clinton deficit-reduction plan] will cost jobs, not create them."*

Senator Pete Domenici, June 1993. In fact, more than 10 million jobs were created during Clinton's first term.

*"Creating a Government That Works Better and Costs Less."*

Title of a 1994 report by Vice President Al Gore, which cost taxpayers $4 per copy to print—$3.10 more than the 90 cents allowed for a standard government report.

*"If I had to bet today on one person for the Republican presidential nomination, I'd put my money on Colin Powell."*

Conservative political pundit William Kristol, September 1995.

*"We happen to believe, despite the polls, that Bill Clinton will lose to any Republican who doesn't drool on stage."*

*Wall Street Journal*, October 1995.

**" "**

*"The last time I checked, the Constitution said 'of the people, by the people, and for the people.' That's what the Declaration of Independence said."*

President Bill Clinton, 1996. Actually, the phrase in question is from the Gettysburg Address.

*"I share your view that the urgent problem of species extinction and the conservation of biological diversity should be addressed. The first step in saving any plant or animal from extinction is to become aware of and respect the fragile ecosystems that make up our environment."*

Vice President Al Gore, 1996, in a letter to a Dallas couple who complained about the elimination of the "Texas Eagle." Gore didn't realize the "Texas Eagle" was an Amtrak train connecting Dallas to Chicago and the West Coast.

*"I was very clearly asked to do the job of being the chief spokesman for the party. I could not do fund-raising."*

Senator Christopher Dodd, February 1997, two months before he admitted to raising money for the party.

**" "**

*"McKinley has no more backbone than a chocolate eclair."*

Theodore Roosevelt, 1898, ridiculing the notion that President William McKinley would go to war against Spain, which he soon after did.

# 5

# *Might Makes Wrong*

## Moronic miscues about war

*"Moscow deserted! A most unlikely event."*

Napoleon Bonaparte, 1812, before entering the evacuated city, which had been set ablaze by fleeing Russians.

*"Our flag still waves proudly from the walls."*

U.S. commander at the Alamo W. Barret Travis, 1836, in his last message before his entire garrison was wiped out by Mexican troops.

*"There is no doubt that Jefferson Davis and the other leaders of the South have made an army . . . they have made a nation."*

British Parliament leader William Gladstone, 1865, shortly before the South collapsed.

*"War is the greatest game on earth."*

The 1890s Princeton University football star John Prentiss Poe Jr., who was killed in action during World War I.

*"We are not interested in the possibilities of defeat. They do not exist."*

British Queen Victoria, 1900, commenting on the Boer War in South Africa, which England lost.

*"Everyone spoke of the possibility of conflict involving all of Europe, but no one here really believed that such a thing was likely to come about."*

*New York Times* financial columnist, June 1914, describing the mood in Europe after the assassination of Austrian Archduke Franz Ferdinand. Within a month, World War I had begun.

*"You will be home before the leaves have fallen from the trees."*

German kaiser Wilhelm II, August 1914, to his troops at the beginning of World War I, which went on for four years.

*"Bullets have little stopping power against the horse."*

British general Sir Douglas Haig, 1914, on the advantages of the cavalry.

*"There will be no war."*

> President Woodrow Wilson, January 1917,
> six months before the U.S. entered World
> War I.

*"The culminating and final war for human liberty."*

> President Woodrow Wilson, January 1918,
> predicting that World War I would be the
> last global war.

*"I hope we may say that thus, this fateful morning, came to an end all wars."*

British Prime Minister David Lloyd George, November 1918, upon the end of World War I.

*"Nobody now fears that a Japanese fleet could deal an unexpected blow on our Pacific possessions. . . . Radio makes surprise impossible."*

U.S. Navy Secretary Josephus Daniels, 1922, nineteen years before Japan's surprise attack on Pearl Harbor.

*"It is about as unthinkable that we should enter armed conflict with our nearest neighbors across the Pacific as it is that we should go to war with one of our nearest neighbors across the Atlantic."*

Thomas Lamont, director of the Japan Society of America, speaking in 1928 about the unlikelihood that the U.S. and Japan would ever fight a war.

## "Mistreatment of Jews in Germany may be considered virtually eliminated."

Secretary of State Cordell Hull, 1933.
Within a decade, virtually the entire Jewish population of Germany, and Europe, would be destroyed.

## "Believe me, Germany is unable to wage war."

British Prime Minister David Lloyd George, 1934.

*"Whoever lights the torch of war in Europe can wish for nothing but chaos."*

German chancellor Adolf Hitler, May 1935, dismissing the notion that Germany wanted war.

*"Germany has no desire to attack any country in Europe."*

British Prime Minister David Lloyd George, 1936.

*"A Japanese attack on Pearl Harbor is a strategic impossibility."*

Author George Fielding Eliot, 1938.

*"I have no more territorial ambitions in Europe."*

Adolf Hitler, 1938, three months before invading Poland.

*"For the second time in our history, a British Prime Minister has returned from Germany bringing peace with honor. I believe it is peace for our time. . . . Go home and get some sleep."*

British Prime Minister Neville Chamberlain, 1938.

*"It has been assumed, in my opinion erroneously, that Japan covets these islands."*

General Douglas MacArthur, 1939, ridiculing rumors that Japan would invade the Philippines, which is exactly what happened.

"An alliance with Germany and Italy . . .
what possible meaning could that have?"

Japanese prince Kinmochi Saionji, 1939.
The alliance meant World War II.

"My feeling and belief is that we are not
going to have a war. Germany isn't ready
for it. . . . I have my own sources of
information."

Senator William E. Borah, ranking
Republican member of the Senate Foreign
Relations Committee, July 1939, six weeks
before Germany invaded Poland.

**"  "**

*"In three weeks, England will have her neck wrung like a chicken."*

French military commander Maxime Weygand, June 1940, assessing England's chances in a war against Nazi Germany. Some 250 weeks later, it was the Germans who were defeated.

*"I have said this before, but I shall say it again and again and again; your boys are not going to be sent into any foreign wars."*

President Franklin D. Roosevelt, 1940, before the U.S. entered World War II.

*"The United States will not be a threat to us for decades."*

Adolf Hitler, November 1940.

*"No matter what happens, the U.S. Navy is not going to be caught napping."*

Secretary of the Navy Frank Knox, December 4, 1941, three days before the Japanese surprise attack on Pearl Harbor.

*"The bomb will never go off, and I speak as an expert in explosives."*

Admiral William Leahy, circa 1944, commenting on the Manhattan Project.

*"Though neutral during WW II, Switzerland favored the Allied cause."*

Inscription on a watch given in 1946 to President Harry Truman by the citizens of Geneva. In fact, the Swiss helped finance the Nazi war effort.

"*Among the really difficult problems of the world, the [Arab-Israeli conflict] is one of the simplest and most manageable.*"

Newspaper columnist Walter Lippmann, 1947, one year before the founding of the State of Israel. There have been five major Arab-Israeli wars since.

*"No commander in the history of war has had more complete and admirable support than I have during the Korean War."*

General Douglas MacArthur, October 1950, six months before he was fired as head of U.S. Armed Forces in Korea.

*"We will bury you."*

Soviet premier Nikita Khrushchev, 1959, to Vice President Richard Nixon.

*"We keep a vigil of peace around the world."*

Vice President Lyndon B. Johnson, May 1963, even as the U.S. was sending military advisers to South Vietnam.

*"It is inconceivable that the Viet Cong could ever defeat the armed forces of South Vietnam."*

General William Westmoreland, newly appointed commander of U.S. Forces in South Vietnam, April 1964.

"We are not about to send American boys nine or ten thousand miles away from home to do what Asian boys ought to be doing for themselves."

President Lyndon B. Johnson, 1964, on Vietnam.

"Our one desire . . . is that the people of Southeast Asia be left in peace to work out their own destinies in their own way."

President Lyndon B. Johnson, 1964, even as he was sending more military advisers to Vietnam.

*"I believe there is a light at the end of what has been a long and lonely tunnel."*

President Lyndon B. Johnson, September 1966, referring to the conflict in Vietnam, seven long and lonely years before it actually ended.

*"We have reached an important point when the end begins to come into view."*

General William Westmoreland, November 1967, six years before the actual end to the Vietnam conflict.

*"We will drive them into the sea."*

Egyptian president Gamal Abdel Nasser, 1968, referring to the State of Israel.

**" "**

*"I want to see peace and prosperity and happiness in my country, and I think we are going about it in the best way."*

Provisional Irish Republican Army leader Joe Cahill, 1971.

# 6

# *Humble Opinions*

Crackpot criticism in art, literature, film, and music

*"Far too noisy, my dear Mozart. Far too many notes."*

Austrian emperor Joseph II, 1786, after hearing the first performance of Mozart's opera *The Marriage of Figaro*.

*"We fancy that any real child might be more puzzled than enchanted by this stiff, overwrought story."*

*Children's Books* review of Lewis Carroll's *Alice in Wonderland*, 1865.

*"What a giftless bastard."*

Composer Pyotr Tchaikovsky, 1886,
referring to rival Johannes Brahms.

*"A sheer dead pull from start to finish."*

*Century Magazine* book review of Charles
Dickens's *Tale of Two Cities*, 1897.

*"I'm sorry, Mr. Kipling, but you just don't understand how to use the English language."*

Publisher's rejection letter, 1889, to *Jungle Book* author Rudyard Kipling.

*"This can only end in suicide. One day, Picasso will be found hanging behind the Demoiselles."*

Painter André Derain, circa 1910, on rival Pablo Picasso's *Les Demoiselles d'Avignon*, widely considered to be the renowned painter's breakthrough painting.

"Possibly some might call it a feminist novel . . . but we are sure Miss Cather had nothing so inartistic in mind."

New York Times book review of Willa Cather's O Pioneers!, 1913, widely thought to be one of the most important feminist novels ever written.

"So this is a book of the season only."

New York Herald Tribune book review of F. Scott Fitzgerald's The Great Gatsby, 1925.

*"Who the hell wants to hear actors talk?"*

Movie mogul and Warner Brothers founder Harry Warner, 1927.

*"Can't act. Can't sing. Balding. Can dance a little."*

MGM executive, 1929, about Fred Astaire's screen test.

"Gone with the Wind *is going to be the biggest flop in Hollywood history.*"

Gary Cooper, 1937, after turning down the role of Rhett Butler.

"No legs, no jokes, no chance."

Producer Mike Todd, 1943, predicting a quick demise of the new Broadway musical *Oklahoma!*, which played for a then-record 2,212 performances.

*"It is impossible to sell animal stories in the U.S.A."*

Publisher's rejection letter, 1945, of George Orwell's *Animal Farm*.

*"The girl doesn't, it seems to me, have a special perception or feeling which would lift that book above the curiosity level."*

Publisher's rejection letter, 1952, of Anne Frank's diary.

*"You cannot show a pregnant woman on television."*

Biow advertising agency executive, 1953, telling Desi Arnaz that it would be a mistake to have his wife, Lucille Ball, shown pregnant on their show *I Love Lucy*. Little Ricky's birth, of course, was one of the highest-rated television shows ever.

*"You ain't going nowhere . . . son. You ought to go back to driving a truck."*

Grand Ole Opry manager Jim Denny, 1954, firing Elvis Presley after one performance.

*"With your voice, nobody is going to let you broadcast."*

CBS producer Don Hewitt, 1958, to Barbara Walters.

*"Any literary merit the book may have is far outweighed by the pornographic and smutty passages."*

Postmaster General Arthur Summerfield, 1959, banning D. H. Lawrence's *Lady Chatterley's Lover*. A month later, a federal judge overruled his decision.

*"There's gotta be a better way to make a living."*

Tonight Show host Jack Paar, February 11, 1960, before walking off a live broadcast after just three minutes. A month later Paar returned.

*"We don't like their sound. Groups of guitars are on their way out."*

Decca Recording Company, 1962, upon turning down the Beatles.

"Reagan doesn't have the presidential look."

United Artists studio executive, 1964.

"The screen soon overflows with so much brotherhood [and] piety [it will make you] retch."

Newsweek magazine, 1964, panning the soon-to-be hit movie *Lilies of the Field*, for which Sidney Poitier became the first black man to win an Oscar for Best Actor.

"They've got their own groups. What are we going to give them that they don't already have?"

Paul McCartney, 1964, anticipating the Beatles' arrival in the U.S.

"They know it's a lot of nonsense. [In another month] America will have had its giggle and once more will be worrying about Castro and Khrushchev."

*New York Daily* news critic Anthony Burton, February 11, 1964, dismissing Beatlemania.

*"Malefic and sick."*

> *New York Times* movie critic Bosley
> Crowther, 1964, reviewing *Dr. Strangelove,*
> widely considered one of the best films ever
> made.

*"Hey, kids! I want you to tiptoe into your parents' bedrooms, look in their pockets for all the green pieces of paper with the pictures of guys in beards, and send them to Soupy Sales at channel 5 in New York."*

Comedian Soupy Sales, 1965, in the closing minute of his television show. The controversy over his ad-lib caused the show's syndicator to take the program off the air temporarily.

## *"Get rid of the pointed ears guy."*

NBC television executive to *Star Trek* creator Gene Roddenberry, 1966, recommending the new show eliminate the Vulcan character Mr. Spock.

## *"Psychedelic Uncle Tom."*

*Esquire* magazine review of rock-and-roll legend Jimi Hendrix, 1967.

*"It's pretty thin, son. I don't think people will follow it."*

Henry Fonda, 1969, commenting to son Peter about his new film—*Easy Rider*—which became an instant hit.

*"I assure you Marlon Brando will not appear in this film."*

Paramount Studios president Stanley Jaffe, circa 1970, on the role of Vito Corleone in *The Godfather*. Brando won an Oscar for his performance of the part.

*"Boring and predictable."*

Time magazine, 1971, panning the future television hit show *All in the Family*.

*"Even an offbeat showcase needs quality."*

New York Times review, 1975, panning *Saturday Night Live*.

"We're going to make everybody forget the Beatles."

Bee Gees singer Barry Gibb, 1976, on his group's movie version of the Beatles' *Sgt. Pepper's Lonely Hearts Club Band.*

"I'm fifty now, and I am sure I won't be doing the Tonight Show *in ten years. I doubt if I'll be doing it at fifty-five."*

Johnny Carson, 1976, who stayed on the job until he was sixty-six.

*"They all thought I'd be the first to go. I was one of the live-fast, die-young, leave-a-good-looking-corpse types, you know. But I guess they were wrong."*

Comedian John Belushi, 1978, playing an elderly version of himself in a short film on *Saturday Night Live*. Four years later, the thirty-three-year-old Belushi died of a drug overdose.

*"Late Night With David Letterman has become a creaking, facetious, contrivance—a choo-choo forever wobbling off the tracks."*

New York critic James Wolcott, 1983, reviewing what was to become one of the most popular late-night TV shows of all time.

*"A flash in the pan."*

Billboard magazine, 1983, in a review of Madonna.

*"That's what I'm going to do—kick Jay's ass."*

Former talk show host Arsenio Hall, 1992, predicting his show's triumph over the *Tonight Show* and Jay Leno. He was wrong.

*"We will make it work. You can take it to the bank."*

CBS newsman Dan Rather, May 1993, on splitting his anchor job with Connie Chung. Two years later Chung was fired.

*"Her involvement has had a very adverse impact on her career because she's unwilling to exploit the situation."*

Attorney Larry Stein, 1996, speaking about his client, O. J. Simpson's ex-girlfriend Paula Barbieri, who later signed a $3 million book deal.

*"For God's sake, definitely I didn't write it."*

Writer Joe Klein, 1996, denying to the *New York Times* that he wrote the novel *Primary Colors*.

*"I'm telling you, I didn't write it."*

Joe Klein, 1996, denying to the *Washington Post* that he wrote the novel *Primary Colors*.

**" "**

*"It's not me. I didn't do it. This is silly."*

Writer Joe Klein, February 1996, denying to CBS News that he wrote the novel *Primary Colors*. He admitted it five months later.

# 7

# *Worst Feet Forward*

**Stumbling statements
from the world of sports**

*"Football isn't meant to be played for money. Stay away from professional football."*

University of Illinois football coach Bob Zuppke, 1918, to future pro football star Red Grange.

*"When autumn comes and the leaves fall off the trees, I'll be on the football field."*

Legendary Notre Dame football coach Knute Rockne, 1930, who died in a plane crash in March 1931.

## *"Is Brooklyn still in the league?"*

New York Giants manager Bill Terry, 1934, dismissing his club's cross-town rivals, the Dodgers. Brooklyn exacted revenge at the end of that season by beating the Giants and preventing them from winning the pennant.

## *"I'll moider de bum."*

Boxer Tony Galento, 1939, referring to his upcoming match with Joe Louis. Da bum moidered Galento.

*"If Stanford wins a single game with that crazy formation, you can throw all the football I ever knew into the Pacific Ocean."*

Legendary football coach Pop Warner, on Stanford's decision to use the then-unusual T-formation, 1940. Stanford won nine games that season and finished second in the nation.

*"That kid can't play baseball."*

Milwaukee Braves minor league manager Tommy Holmes, 1952, appraising Henry Aaron, who went on to break Babe Ruth's all-time record for home runs.

*"My roots are in Brooklyn, so why should I move?"*

Brooklyn Dodgers owner Walter O'Malley, mid-1950s, denying rumors that he would move his club to Los Angeles, which he did after the 1957 season.

*"This team of ours is the worst I've ever seen in training."*

Detroit Lions coach Buddy Parker, 1957, upon quitting before the season—and before the Lions went on to win the NFL title.

*"Nobody is going to pay to come out and watch your players run up and down the court in their underwear."*

Los Angeles businessman Jerry Adelman, 1960, to L.A. Lakers general manager Lou Mohs.

*"Unfortunately, I don't think I'll ever get the chance and there's nothing in the world that can change that."*

Former Yankees shortstop Billy Martin, 1961, on his chances of ever becoming a manager. Martin, of course, went on to win two World Series as Yankees manager in the 1970s.

*"He won't make it."*

Chicago Cubs scout Gordon Goldsberry,
1966, evaluating future Hall of Fame
pitcher Tom Seaver.

*"I'll be commissioner when the sun goes
down tonight, and I'll be commissioner
when the sun comes up Friday."*

American Football League commissioner
Joe Foss, 1966, who resigned an hour and a
half later.

*"The New York Jets would do well to trade Joe Namath."*

New York Times football analyst William Wallace, August 1968, the season in which Namath would lead the Jets to victory in the Super Bowl.

*"Baseball is doomed."*

Social philosopher Marshall McLuhan, 1969.

*"He'll never be more than a 13–14 game winner. He's a mama's boy."*

Pitching coach Johnny Sain, early 1970s, appraising Tommy John, who became one of the best pitchers of his era.

*"Preempt Doris Day? Are you out of your mind?"*

CBS president Bob Wood, 1970, turning down the chance to broadcast *Monday Night Football*.

*"We are confident that if the city acquires Yankee Stadium and completes its plans for modernization of the stadium, the New York Giants will remain in New York City."*

New York mayor John Lindsay, 1971, on plans to keep the Giants in the Big Apple. The team moved to New Jersey seven years later.

*"Mr. Finley has told me that I'll die in his green and gold."*

Oakland A's slugger Reggie Jackson, 1973, referring to A's owner Charles Finley's promise that Jackson would always be on the team. He soon left.

*"I'll stick to building ships."*

New York Yankees owner George Steinbrenner, 1973, promising not to interfere in day-to-day operations after buying the team.

*"The time may have come to say good-bye to Muhammad Ali."*

Broadcaster Howard Cosell, 1974, predicting Ali's loss to heavyweight boxing champ George Foreman in their title bout in Zaire. Ali won.

*"There has never been any violence in the NHL."*

National Hockey League president Clarence Campbell, 1974.

*"This time we're going to win the Super Bowl."*

Minnesota Vikings quarterback Fran Tarkenton, 1976. That season, the team lost its fourth title game, to the Oakland Raiders.

*" . . . our league has never been in better shape."*

Gordie Howe, 1976, commenting on the state of the soon-to-be-defunct World Hockey Association.

*"We've come to the mountain and Muhammad must fall."*

Note on blackboard at boxer Earnie Shavers's training camp before his 1977 fight with Muhammad Ali, who won the bout.

*"Bobick is a very durable fighter."*

Boxer Ken Norton, 1977, before his first-round victory over rival Duane Bobick.

*"Doc Ellis is not going anywhere."*

New York Yankees owner George
Steinbrenner, 1977, denying reports that
Ellis would be traded. A week later he was.

*"It is extremely doubtful if any coach
active today will even come close to
approaching [Amos Alonzo] Stagg's 314
victories."*

Sportswriters Mervin Hyman and Gordon
White Jr., 1977, five years before Stagg's
record was broken by Alabama coach Paul
"Bear" Bryant.

*"Any company that doesn't let its employees off on Bronco Day should be ashamed of itself."*

Colorado governor Richard Lamm, 1977, declaring a holiday when the Denver Broncos won the AFC league championship. Lamm canceled the day off soon after when he learned it would cost the state $5 million.

*"Sparky will absolutely not be traded."*

New York Yankees general manager Al Rosen, 1978. In fact, Sparky Lyle was traded later that season.

*"I'm twenty-four and I think I'll get a lot more opportunities."*

Golfer Jerry Pate, 1978, after losing one of professional golf's major championships in 1978. Pate never won another.

*"Leonard will kiss the floor of the ring because he talks too much."*

Boxer Roberto Duran, 1980, before his second fight with Sugar Ray Leonard, who won.

*"No man was great enough to come back three times. I will do it a fourth time because it's there."*

Boxer Muhammad Ali, 1981, before his bid to win the heavyweight title one more time. He lost to Canadian champ Trevor Berbick in ten rounds.

*"Bob Lemon is going to be our manager all year . . . I swear on my heart."*

New York Yankees owner George Steinbrenner, 1982. Lemon was fired fourteen games into the season.

*"There is no doubt that soccer will one day challenge football and baseball as the number one sport in America."*

North American Soccer League commissioner Phil Woosnam, 1982.

*"We expect within two or three years to have virtual parity with the NFL."*

New York real estate tycoon Donald Trump, 1983, on on his move into sports with the New Jersey Generals of the upstart U.S. Football League. The USFL folded three years later.

*"He'll never be any good."*

Baltimore Colts owner Robert Irsay, 1983, evaluating future Pro Bowl and Super Bowl champion quarterback John Elway.

*"I will not let that happen again."*

Kansas State football coach Stan Parrish, 1987, after his team finished the season without a victory. They repeated that feat the next year.

*"For years people called us the armpit of the San Gabriel Valley. Today we're the crown jewel."*

Irwindale, California, mayor Xavier Hermosillo, 1987, after the Oakland Raiders announced they would move there. The Raiders soon changed their minds.

*"In twenty years of tournament golf involving amateurs, I've never been hit by a ball."*

Golfer Hale Irwin, 1989, one week before he was hit on the head at the Los Angeles Open tournament.

*"I have more faith in my wife than to bump off her competition."*

Tonya Harding's husband Jeff Gillooly, January 1994, less than two months before he pleaded guilty to assaulting Harding's skating rival Nancy Kerrigan.

*"As long as I own the Cleveland Browns they will remain in Cleveland."*

Cleveland Browns owner Art Modell, 1993. Modell moved the franchise to Baltimore in 1996.

*"I am looking forward to becoming a Marine with the same determination and commitment that made me a champion."*

Boxer Riddick Bowe, 1997, before leaving boot camp after three days.

*"Student-Athletes shall be amateurs in an intercollegiate sport, and . . . should be protected from exploitation by professional and commercial enterprise."*

From the National Collegiate Athletic Association manual, which later allows that "racing bibs and similar competition identification materials [e.g., bowl-game patches] worn by participants may include the name of the corporate sponsor of the competition."

# 8

# *Better Left Unsaid*

## Infamous last words

*"Am I my brother's keeper?"*

Cain, Genesis 4:9, denying responsibility
for the murder of his brother Abel.

*"All men are created equal."*

From the Declaration of Independence, July
4, 1776, by Thomas Jefferson, a slaveowner
until his death fifty years later.

*"If there be one principle more deeply rooted than any other in the mind of every American, it is that we should have nothing to do with conquest."*

President Thomas Jefferson, 1791, before, among other conquests, the Mexican-American War and the great Indian wars.

*"Don't give up the ship."*

U.S. Navy captain and commander of the *Chesapeake* James Lawrence, 1813, in a battle with British sea forces. He did, and died.

*"I will give him . . . such an illumination as this world has never seen."*

A priest from the Jesuit Church of LaCompania, Chile, 1863, promising a glorious pageant for the visiting representative from the Pope. Unfortunately, the church burned down before the pageant began.

*"Beyond a doubt all stories about large bodies of Indians being here are the merest bosh."*

General George Armstrong Custer, 1876, a few weeks before he and his troops were massacred by a large body of Sioux Indians at the Little Big Horn river.

*"You will never amount to very much."*

A Munich teacher to ten-year-old Albert Einstein, 1889.

*"I have no enemies. Why should I fear?"*

President William McKinley, August 1901,
a few days before his assassination.

*"You bet I will pull through."*

Financier J. P. Morgan, 1913, upon
emerging from a coma. Within minutes he
was dead.

*"I am very happy in the Senate and much prefer to remain there. I do not believe I could be happy as president. I don't want it."*

Senator Warren G. Harding, 1920, before running for and winning the job of president.

*"Thousand year Reich."*

Slogan, circa 1930s, predicting the length of Nazi Party rule in Germany, which in fact lasted twelve years.

*"The federal government must and shall quit this business of relief."*

President Franklin D. Roosevelt, January 1935, before going on to create the largest relief projects in U.S. history.

*"We shall not capitulate—no, never!"*

German chancellor Adolf Hitler, 1939, six years before Germany surrendered and Hitler killed himself.

*"Don't worry about it. . . . It's nothing."*

U.S. Navy Lt. Kermit Tyler, December 7, 1941, upon being informed that radar had just picked up a large formation of planes heading for Hawaii. It was, of course, the first wave of the Japanese attack on Pearl Harbor.

*"It is significant that despite the claims of air enthusiasts no battleship has yet been sunk by bombs."*

Caption under the photograph of the battleship USS *Arizona* in the program for the annual Army-Navy football game, November 29, 1941. Eight days later Japanese bombers sank the *Arizona* at Pearl Harbor.

*"Fireproof."*

Designation given by Atlanta fire inspectors, 1946, to the Winecoff Hotel, which shortly thereafter burned to the ground.

*"The largest, safest, and most modern hotel west of New York."*

Promotional copy for Chicago's La Salle Hotel, which went up in flames on June 5, 1946.

*"You can't say the people of Dallas haven't given you a nice welcome."*

Mrs. John Connally, wife of the governor of Texas, to John Kennedy, November 22, 1963, just prior to Kennedy's assassination.

*"We have a free press . . . honest elections. . . . In all this part of the world, where will democratic ways work if they fail here?"*

Philippines president Ferdinand Marcos, 1967, five years before declaring martial law to remain in power and nineteen years before being overthrown for corruption.

*"Let me be quite blunt. Our fighting men are not going to be worn down. Our mediators are not going to be talked down. And our allies are not going to be let down."*

President Richard Nixon, May 1969, on the Vietnam War.

*"I have often been accused of putting my foot in my mouth, but I will never put my hand in your pockets."*

Vice President Spiro Agnew, 1969. Agnew eventually resigned for taking political kickbacks.

*"I'm going to live to be one hundred."*

Health author Jerome Rodale, 1971, who
died the next day at age fifty-one.

*"I have no intention whatever of walking
away from the job I was elected to do."*

President Richard Nixon, November 1973,
nine months before he resigned from office.

*"I don't need bodyguards."*

Union leader Jimmy Hoffa, 1975, nine months before his abduction and murder.

*" . . . a survivor who is frustrating the curse of the Oscar."*

*Washington Post* profile in September 1978 of actor Gig Young, who shot his wife and himself to death a month later.

*"It's too early for a Polish pope."*

Polish cardinal Karol Wojtyla, October 1978, two days before he was elected Pope.

*"We encouraged him [the shah of Iran] to hang firm and count on our backing."*

President Jimmy Carter, November 1978, shortly before the shah was overthrown.

*"Nobody knows more about this mountain than Harry, and it don't dare blow up on him."*

Retiree Harry Truman, May 1980, explaining why he wouldn't evacuate his home near Mt. St. Helens, Washington, which erupted on May 18.

*"I'll keep you safe, kids. I swear to God."*

Dialogue to be spoken by actor Vic Morrow, 1982, as he rescued two Vietnamese children in *Twilight Zone: The Movie*. Before the scene was shot, however, Morrow and the two child actors were killed in an on-set accident.

*"I have just one father. I want to make peace with him."*

Singer Marvin Gaye, 1984, shortly before he got into a fight with his dad, who shot and killed his son.

*"Can you believe this crap?"*

Actor Jon-Erik Hexum, October 1984, before firing a gun loaded with blanks during a break in filming his television show, *Cover-Up*. The impact from the blast put Hexum in a coma, and he died six days later.

---

*"You don't understand. They don't kidnap
journalists."*

Journalist Terry Anderson, 1985, less than
a week before he was kidnapped by Arab
terrorists.

*"I am not a mercenary."*

Former Green Beret and singer Barry Sadler,
1986. In 1988 Sadler was shot by an
unknown assailant while he was reportedly
training Nicaraguan contras in Guatemala.
He died of his wounds a year later.

---

*"The fact is that I don't like publicity. I absolutely hate doing an interview."*

Tycoon Donald Trump, 1987, in an interview with *People* magazine. Trump eventually put his name on a casino, an airline, and a bicycle race, in addition to the Trump Tower in New York City.

" "

*"You've got to get rid of self-consciousness and get full of God-consciousness."*

Televangelist Jimmy Swaggart, April 1987. The next year Swaggart's ministry was rocked by scandal when his relationship with a prostitute was discovered.

*"I've got Bush by the balls."*

Panamanian leader Manuel Noriega, 1988, on George Bush. Two years later Noriega was behind bars.

*"The rich and famous should be judged differently. The city couldn't live with the little people's tax money."*

Actress Zsa Zsa Gabor, 1989, claiming that she shouldn't be held responsible for slapping a police officer after a routine arrest. In fact, she was found guilty.

*"Taxes are for the little people."*

Billionairess Leona Helmsley, circa mid-1980s. Helmsley was subsequently convicted on charges of tax evasion.

*"I have flown ValuJet. ValuJet is a safe airline."*

Transportation Secretary Federico Peña, May 1996, a month before shutting the troubled airline down.

*"You won't catch us."*

Henri Paul, who was driving Princess Diana on the night of her death in a car crash in 1997, to photographers, as alleged in the *New York Daily News*.

# 9

# *Wishful Thinking*

**There's no bigger fool than an optimist**

*"There is every reason to believe that our system will soon attain the highest degree of perfection of which human institutions are capable."*

President James Monroe, 1820.

*"Slavery has not created interests in the South contrary to those of the North."*

French politician and writer Alexis de Tocqueville, 1835.

*"Happily a matter of but little practical importance."*

President James Buchanan, 1857, describing the debate about slavery.

*"Assassination can be no more guarded against than death by lightning and it is best not to worry about either."*

President James A. Garfield, 1881, who was soon after assassinated.

*"In 1993, the world will have become equalized in every respect, even to dire monotony."*

Magazine publishing magnate Miriam Leslie, 1893. Anybody bored yet?

*"The citizens who live in the next century are not going to pay two cents for a letter postage stamp. The price will be reduced to one cent."*

Postmaster General Thomas L. James, 1893.

*"All theology will be conceded to be mythology."*

Noted journalist, author, and lawyer Van Buren Denslow, 1893, speculating on how things would look in 1993.

*"Free delivery will be universal."*

Postmaster General John Wanamaker, 1893, predicting how the U.S. postal system would look in 1993.

*"Far more religion than now. . . . The spirit of religion dominant."*

> Newspaper columnist and clergyman Thomas DeWitt Talmage, 1893, predicting the role of theology one hundred years in the future.

*"One hundred years from now, the people of the United States will be traveling at a rate of 100 miles an hour—on electrical railways."*

> Secretary of the Treasury Charles Foster, 1893.

*"People have got to know whether or not their president is a crook. Well, I'm not a crook. I've earned everything I've got."*

Richard M. Nixon, 1974, about the Watergate burglary of Democratic National Headquarters.

*"One hundred years hence, I think the President of the United States will have much less work on his hands than he has now."*

U.S. Army paymaster and former personal secretary to President Benjamin Harrison, Elijah Halford, 1893.

*"Men will grow wiser, better, and purer in the years to come."*

Senator William A. Peffer, 1893, predicting how things would look in 1993.

*"Transcontinental mails will be forwarded by means of pneumatic tubes."*

Renowned writer and naturalist Felix Oswald, 1893, predicting how the world would look in 1993.

*"Not just another war—it is the last war."*

British historian and author H. G. Wells, 1914, speaking about the first—and hardly the last—world war.

*"I have seen over into the future, and it works."*

American journalist Lincoln Steffens, 1919, upon returning from a trip to post-revolution Russia.

*"The bonds . . . which are always drawing North and South Ireland together will prove too powerful for the bigots and revolutionaries."*

Irish journalist J. R. Devlin, 1925.

*"England is at last ripe for revolution."*

Russian Communist leader Leon Trotsky, 1925, predicting the overthrow of the British government.

*"In thirty years the United States will see the end of dire poverty, distress, and unnecessary suffering."*

Real estate mogul and philanthropist August Heckscher, 1930. Still waiting.

*"I do not believe in the probability of anything much worse than mustard gas being produced."*

British scientist J. B. S. Haldane, 1937, on the future of weaponry.

*"Sidewalks will be elevated—you'll walk and shop above Main Street, actually cross over it."*

Futurist Norman Bel Geddes, 1937, predicting what downtown would look like in a typical U.S. city by 1960.

*"No enemy bomber can reach the Ruhr."*

Nazi leader Hermann Goering, 1939, on the impossibility that enemy airplanes could penetrate into Germany.

*"It's a phony war."*

French prime minister Edouard Daladier, 1939, on the beginning of World War II.

*"In the course of thirty years the human race will have been biologically restored. It will come into the world without any trace of fascist distortion."*

Austrian psychiatrist Wilhelm Reich, 1946.

*"[Television] won't be able to hold on to any market it captures after the first six months. People will soon get tired of staring at a plywood box every night."*

Twentieth Century-Fox studio boss Darryl F. Zanuck, 1946.

*"The housewife of 2000 can do her daily cleaning with a garden hose."*

Popular Mechanics magazine, 1950, predicting that U.S. homes and all their furnishings would be made of plastic by the end of the century.

*"Employers are going to love this generation. They aren't going to press many grievances. They are going to be easy to handle. There aren't going to be any riots."*

University of California chancellor Clark Kerr, 1959.

*"The class war is obsolete."*

British prime minister Harold Macmillan, 1959, on the relationship between the rich and the poor.

*"I found nothing but progress and hope for the future."*

Secretary of Defense Robert McNamara, 1963, upon returning from a visit to Vietnam.

*"I'm not going to lose Vietnam."*

President Lyndon B. Johnson, 1963.

*"Within ten to twenty years' time we could have a robot that will completely eliminate all routine operations around the house and remove the drudgery from human life."*

British mechanical engineering professor Meredith Woolridge Thring, 1964.

*"The major part of the U.S. Military task in Vietnam can be completed by the end of 1965."*

Secretary of Defense Robert McNamara, 1965. He was off by just eight years.

*"It won't be a convention, but a coronation."*

Political strategist and aide Frank Mankiewicz, 1972, upon George McGovern's nomination as the Democratic presidential candidate. McGovern went on to lose forty-eight of fifty states to Richard Nixon.

*"There is no Soviet domination of Eastern Europe."*

President Gerald Ford, 1976.

*"A normal aberration."*

Three Mile Island nuclear power plant spokesman Jack Herbein, 1979, in the early stages of the most serious nuclear disaster in U.S. history.

*" . . . at this time the risk of contracting this immunosuppressive agent is minimal and C.D.C. is not recommending any change in blood-product use."*

National Hemophilia Foundation statement, July 1982, on the chances of catching the AIDS virus. In fact, roughly 90 percent of severe hemophiliacs in the U.S. were infected.

*"Within the next fifteen years, almost everyone will have an integrated home computer with which they can monitor their health from home, diagnose themselves, and take care of themselves."*

General Health president James Bernstein, 1986.

*"High standards start here. Rigourous Graduation Requirement. Mathematics and Writing Proficiencey Exams."*

Newspaper ad for Milwaukee's public school system, 1997, in which the words "rigorous" and "proficiency" were misspelled.

*"In 1940, a one-pound loaf of bread cost 8 cents, and in 1995 cost 79 cents; a half-gallon of milk went from 25 cents to $1.43 in the same period; and a first-class postage stamp went from 3 cents to 32 cents. Which, bottom line, means that first-class postage rates remained well below the rate of inflation."*

U.S. Postal Service ad, 1996. Actually, those figures prove that the price of stamps rose 9 percent faster than the price of bread and 105 percent faster than the price of milk.

*"We've built a yellow brick road to the summit."*

Mountain climber Scott Fischer before a fateful ascent of Mt. Everest in 1996 that resulted in eight deaths, including his own.

# Sources and Bibliography

The quotations in this collection were gleaned from the books listed below, as well as from a variety of publications and periodicals, including (but not limited to) *Entertainment Weekly*, The *National Review*, The *New Republic*, The *New York Times*, *Newsweek*, *People*, *Smart Money* and *Time*. The editor gratefully acknowledges all assistance in compiling the material for this book, especially that of Jason Zweig at *Money*.

Edward Angly. *Oh Yeah?* New York: Viking, 1931.

Louise K. Barnett. *Touched by Fire: The Life, Death, and Mythic Afterlife of George Armstrong Custer*. New York: Henry Holt, 1996.

Edward Behr. *Hirohito: Behind the Myth*. New York: Villard Books, 1989.

Andre Bernard, ed. *Rotten Rejections*. Wainscott, N.Y.: Pushcart Press, 1990.

Wilford Binkley. *President and Congress*. New York: Vintage Books, 1962.

Ivan F. Boesky. *Merger Mania*. New York: Holt, Rinehart and Winston, 1985.

— " " —

Paul F. Boller, Jr. *Quotemanship*. Dallas: Southern Methodist University Press, 1967.

Connie Bruck. *The Predator's Ball*. New York: Simon and Schuster, 1988.

James M. Burns. *Roosevelt: The Soldier of Freedom*. New York: Harcourt Brace Jovanovich, 1970.

Bob Chieger and Pat Sullivan. *Football's Greatest Quotes*. New York: Simon and Schuster, 1990.

Winston Churchill. *Their Finest Hour*. New York: Bantam Books, 1962.

Joseph Corn and Brian Horrigan. *Yesterday's Tomorrows: Past Visions of the American Future*. Baltimore: Johns Hopkins University Press, 1975.

Paul Dickson. *Baseball's Greatest Quotations*. New York: HarperCollins, 1991.

Deborah Davis Eisel and Jill Swanson, eds. *Dictionary of Contemporary Quotations*. New York: John Gordon Burke Publisher, 1981.

Stuart Flexner with Doris Flexner. *The Pessimist's Guide to History*. New York: Hearst Books, 1992.

Frank Friedel. *Franklin D. Roosevelt*. Boston: Little, Brown, 1956.

Elizabeth Frost, ed. *The World Almanac of Presidential Quotations*. New York: Pharos Books, 1988.